The Smell of

Poverty

A Compilation of Life's Story of Poverty

ROYSTON
Publishing

BK Royston Publishing
P. O. Box 4321
Jeffersonville, IN 47131
502-802-5385
http://www.bkroystonpublishing.com
bkroystonpublishing@gmail.com

Cover Design: Shannon Griffin

ISBN: 978-1-946111-55-5

Printed in the United States of America

DEDICATION

This book is dedicated to anyone who has experienced the Smell of Poverty. Our Hope is that even though poverty may be where you started it doesn't have to be your final destination. Take these stories to heart as encouragement, inspiration, and the path to walk away from poverty and live the abundant life forever.

ACKNOWLEDGEMENTS

First, we acknowledge God for giving each write the gift of words to share with the world.

To Shannon Griffin for being the visionary, coordinator, and leader of this project. God bless you in everything your hand touches and your heart imagines.

To all of the authors of this anthology, we thank you for your contribution.

Maurisa Alexis

Talibah Aset

Evangelist Evelyn Baudoin-Glasper

Prophetess Wanakee M. Brown-Belin

Faye Thomas Fulton-Venerable

Shannon Griffin

Adrianne Johnson

Dee Marie Jones

Elizabeth KorKor

William T. Matthews, O.D.

Sue May

Jacqueline McKeever

Raquel Neal

Julia Royston

Raeshal Solomon

Sherry Thompson

To BK Royston Publishing for publishing this work for the world. Let's go!

Table of Contents

THE
SMELL
OF
POVERTY

<u>Maurisa Alexis</u>

Wife, mother, daughter, sister, advocate, and friend.

Maurisa says that God is her guide and the center of her universe; without him, accolades and accomplishments mean nothing.

Maurisa Alexis-Louis is the owner operator of Bay Area Cleaning Professionals, a residential and commercial cleaning company in Baytown, Texas. Maurisa has been an entrepreneur for over 15 years and prides herself in helping families spend more time together by freeing moms from the burdensome tasks of house cleaning to being able to enjoy their home.

Maurisa has served on many boards and chaired various committees for service leagues in the community. Maurisa also was an active participant for the "cleaning for a reason" campaign.

Maurisa's all-time favorite thing to do is spend time with her family, and she enjoys meeting new and exciting people.

The Smell of Poverty

The Definition of POVERTY ACCORDING TO MERRIAM WEBSTER IS *the state of one who lacks a usual or socially acceptable amount of money or material possessions. Other words that can be used to describe poverty are scarcity, dearth, or lack.*

I was born in Trinidad and Tobago W.I., a very beautiful country full of strong and vibrant people. A land full of natural resources. A multicultural country full of delectable food, stout rum, and culture.

My name is Maurisa Alexis-Louis, and this is my poverty story.

I was born in the 1970s; I am the second of three, which makes me the middle child. My sister, Avril, is the oldest, and that leaves my brother, Marlon as the baby. The 1970s were a time for change, and during this time America was experiencing major development, especially in the south. My father at that time was blessed with the opportunity to learn a trade and become a well sought-after craftsman. So much so that he was hired and received a visa to travel to St. Croix in the United States Virgin Islands to work. From there, he was promoted and received an offer with Brown and Root to relocate to Texas, and work in the refineries, which at that time kept welders and other craftsman in high demand.

My parents decided it would be best if my mom stayed in Trinidad until my dad got settled and found housing suitable for a family. During this time, we lived with my maternal grandparents, and it was then I bonded with my grandparents so much so that when my mom traveled to Texas, she left me with them. I didn't mind because they were loving and kind to me, plus staying with them gave me a love for my culture and my country that I would not have gotten had I left the country with my mom and siblings.

My first encounter with poverty was on a trip to the market with my grandfather. I always looked forward to going to the market with my grandfather because I would always return with my favorite snacks. On this trip, I noticed my grandfather was busy counting his change. He made extra efforts to count it twice. He had approximately five dollars in quarters and dimes. It wasn't until we were walking back home that I noticed he would discreetly put ten cents in the pails of disheveled, vagrant men; through the eyes of a child, I just thought they were all drunks and wanted to be on the streets. He gave twenty-five cents to the old women who stood on the street corners. They shared the same appearance as the men except they appeared to be more aggressive with asking for money. Both shared the common fragrance of the street, that down-trodden aroma of poverty. I asked my grandfather why he gave more money to the women and he explained that women usually had someone other than themselves to take care of and men, even if going through a hard time, could get something to do quicker than a woman.

My second encounter with poverty happened when I was 6 years old. I remember looking out of the window and into my neighbors' home. I could see her beating her soon so badly he began bleeding. She cursed him and beat him until I just couldn't watch any more. I asked my grandmother why the neighbor treated her son this way, and she told me to mind my business. I continued watching this event quite frequently, except the beatings would go from one child to the next until she made it to all eight children and then she would start all over again.

I lived with this in my memory bank for so long that my mom got tired of me talking about it! So much so that she explained to me that our neighbor was very angry because her husband traveled to England the very same year I was born and never returned. She became angry and depressed because she had no money and her only other option was to beg for handouts from the community and the government. She was left fending for herself and eight children. I could go on to tell the stories of her children stealing from other families in our village but why? I think I have made my point. Unfortunately, because of her mental status and her financial lack, she ended up abusing her children and eventually having a nervous breakdown and spent the rest of her life in a mental institution. Now eight children were left without a mother or father. I left the country and by the time I returned they were all dispersed among distant family. This memory reeks of the stench of poverty. If I close my eyes and think back, I can still smell a faint tang of this vicious thing called poverty.

When I came to America, I was looking forward to coming to the land of the free and the home of the brave. My dad decided to move to Baytown, Texas, because he needed to be close to the oil refineries. We moved to Texas in the dead of winter and everything seemed so depressed at the time. Texas was so big and during the 70s, it was underdeveloped; thus, there was a lot of wide open area. So you could literally drive for miles upon miles until you got to the next town.

It was a strange environment for me, and I longed to be back on my little island country where everything was familiar. My dreams of America quickly faded when we arrived in this place that we now called home. This placed reeked of pork guts and other unfamiliar smells. It was a trailer park in an area where only African American people lived. You see my dad was also dealing with culture shock. He moved to Texas in the 1970s, which was a time of racial upset. The Blacks here were still living with economic disadvantage. They lacked knowledge, education, and skills necessary to achieve higher wages less they were stuck doing the minimum wage jobs. My dad moved us smack dab in the middle of the Black south with people who looked like us but hated our very existence because we were willing to take jobs that they were insulted by. This is another vivid recollection of poverty and this experience planted a memory in my mind for life. The trailer park had an odor that you could smell from three blocks away. Poor plumbing, sewage, and sanitation systems contributed to this. Rage, sadness, and lack of motivation also subsidized this place of poverty. I came from a third-world country where these same conditions existed; however, because my grandparents were middle class I was sheltered, and because I was a child I had more than the necessary comforts.

To the reader of my poverty story. Please note that these stories I share are not meant to hurt or belittle anyone. It is meant to be used as a tool to shed light on this demographic and ultimately minister to someone who has been through this very same situation.

Jeremiah 29:11 "For I know the plans I have for you,"
declares the Lord, "plans to prosper you and not to
harm you, plans to give you hope and a future." (NIV)

__Talibah Aset__

I am Talibah Aset, life purpose coach, personal branding/marketing consultant and legacy wealth creation specialist. I am also an affiliate of Karatbars International GmbH. I teach women entrepreneurs to brand themselves and create generational wealth by building upon their natural gifts, talents, and abilities and by becoming financially literate and making sound decisions regarding their money, relationships, businesses, and self-care. I am the owner of Elemental Riches: The Golden Legacy, a movement for women away from a legacy of poverty and powerlessness to a legacy of peace, power, and prosperity through paying themselves first and saving in gold.

To connect with Talibah,

email: 999.9AuLife@gmail.com,

visit: www.elementalriches.com or

call: (513) 428-4653

How to Never Be Poor Again

Does poverty even have a smell? Yes, it does. To me, it is the stench of old cigarette butts, dirty laundry that has been sitting around for way too long, mildew from the leaky pipes in the walls that are slowly destroying the house. "The Smell of Poverty" is the suffocating odor of the toilet that is full, because yet again, the water is off. The nuances of the stink may be different for everyone, but for all who have experienced it, it is the reek of lack. It is the odor that comes along with not having enough. I am not sure when I first recognized it in my life, but I know that I am sick and disgusted with it. I suppose I could tell you all about my struggles with poverty as a condition. That is not really my story, though.

You see, I — like most of my peers — have experienced poverty as a state of being or a physical condition. Unlike many of my peers, I have never experienced poverty as a mindset. I have never been tethered to an idea of there not being enough. At best, I could always manifest anything I needed, regardless of the current situation I faced. At worst, I understood that I had not yet learned to create whatever it is that I desired. I have never understood the idea of need, since it is impossible to need what you don't have. Seriously, if you truly needed it, then it must be: that is the law. It is always a matter of perception, and truth is truth only as far as it is perceived.

My story is not one that focused much on the experience of poverty as a condition, but one of accepting the condition and then resolving to release myself from it. There is no condition that can exist in your life without your sanction. I have learned that the first step out of the condition is to first accept that it is you who created it, called it into being. You must figure out why it is that you called the experience to yourself. I have a habit of asking myself, in any situation, "Who do I have to be, to have called this situation into my experience?" There is no way for me to change any circumstance without first accepting ownership of it. Until I own it, I cannot release it.

And so it is with the physical condition of poverty that I called the experience into my life, for the lessons it taught. It has been simply a part of my becoming — nothing more, nothing less. I am not a victim of poverty. I am not bound to it. I appreciate the experience for who I have become because of it. It is because of the condition of poverty that I am fearless and bold. Poverty is a part of the reason I am a great teacher and coach. It is also by way of poverty that I have learned to be compassionate and understanding toward others. The condition of poverty has helped me to understand the difference between cost and value, the importance of delayed gratification, (that there is no such thing as something for nothing), and the pricelessness of investing in myself, my work, and my passions. Poverty has also created a strong desire in me to manage my money well, but not be tied to it, and to see opportunities rather than obstacle. And, as crazy as it seems, it was the condition of poverty that has helped me to develop the skills and attitudes necessary to create true, sustainable, generational wealth.

Because of the condition of poverty, I have learned what money is and what it is not. I know better than to chase profits without backing them up with a long-term store of value. I know that the Federal Reserve Note, we call money, is not lawful money. I also understand that the only, real money that exists is currency grade gold, and so I keep 100% of my savings in gold. I know that it is important to educate my children and grandchildren about how money works. I also know how important it is to give generously, because if I truly believe the world is an abundant place, I have no need to penny pinch or worry about a dollar; either way, there will always be enough wealth for me.

The condition of poverty more than anything has taught me the depth of my personal power, relentlessness of my resolve, and limitlessness of my creativity. It has afforded me the courage to stretch beyond measure to do what others will not and go where they cannot. Today, I have a business that is unique to only me. I am a life purpose coach, personal branding/marketing consultant, and legacy wealth creation specialist. I help women entrepreneurs create and launch kickass brands, balance their work and personal lives, and create a legacy of wealth that can be passed down for generations to come. All for one super low monthly fee. And the best part is I get to give back to them by requiring that the first $60 of their monthly fee be paid to themselves first in a gold savings account. Why? Because I can and because it is important to me for the women I work with to protect themselves financially. I require every one of my clients to save in gold, and to help them I make their savings part of my fee. My business is helping other women grow in every way they can, and my wealth comes from doing so. I can do the work I love without worrying about the amount I am paid because I understand that at the end of the day gold is money, gold is wealth, gold is protection. The great banker, J.P. Morgan said, "Gold is money. Everything else is credit. Once you understand that, you will never be poor again." This is every bit as true today, as it was when he said it. If you want to know about my exit plan from poverty, I would have to say that is to always understand that it is a condition you are experiencing and not a definition of who you are. Understand what you can learn from it. Refuse to be a victim of it and use it to your advantage. And always save in gold.

I am Talibah Aset and I refuse to accept that there exists any force sufficient in power to defeat me — poverty or otherwise.

Evangelist Evelyn Baudoin-Glasper

Born May 14, 1944, in Abbeville, Louisiana, to the late Clifton Campbell, Sr. and the late Iola (Baudoin) George. The oldest of nine siblings: five boys and four girls. She married William Sr., and had two sons, William Jr. and Gregory. She is a grandmother and great-grandmother, president of Sunshine Career Counseling and

Referral Services, Inc., and an independent beauty consultant with Mary Kay. She is listed in the Senior Citizens Resource Guide, which circulates to several parishes throughout Louisiana. From a child, Evangelist Evelyn started working to help support her siblings.

I give thanks to those who made a difference in my childhood: my mother, maternal grandmother, and former teachers. I give appreciation to my husband, sons, and family who inspired me, including my great-grandfather, Anthony Campbell, instilling in us to READ, READ, AND READ. He kept a newspaper under his arms every day, and people thought he was the smartest person in our community. Out of four generations, I was the first to graduate from high school and first to go to college, even though I didn't finish college. I am thankful for my mentors throughout my career: the late Dorothy Mae Taylor, the late

Oretha Castle Haley, Rev. Avery Alexande,r and others who fought through the Civil Rights Era.

MY STORY

When I was six, I picked cotton with my brothers to help pay the rent. It was then that I knew I wanted to make changes to help my family and me have a better life. When it was cotton-picking season, we could not go to school sometimes for weeks or months at a time. I would go to school the first day to get all of my books, attend classes to meet my teachers, and get the assignments. During my lunch break when I was in the cotton fields, I would read and work through class lessons even though I was not in class. I was determined to be at least two or three chapters ahead of the class.

Once I came home from the cotton fields, I had to wash clothes for the family, iron, bathe, and put my younger siblings to bed. Sometimes I had to prepare something for our meals because our mother was working two jobs. Our dad was in my life and that was it. I cannot remember him providing any support to us. While in those cotton fields, I would dream and see myself doing other things and getting out of those fields.

At age 13, there was chaos and unstable conditions with my mother and dad separating, and I didn't want to live with either of them. So I decided to live my dad's mother, who already had a house full of children of her own. Some of my grandmother's children were the same age as me, and some even younger than I was. While living with my grandmother, I did not have time to be a child or teenager. I had to work there and go to my mother's house to work.

When I started doing housework outside of the home, I was being paid sometimes 50¢ or 75¢ a day. A day was early in the morning until sundown. I was not pleased with that, and I decided to live with one of my dad's aunts who lived in Houston, Texas. I thought life would be better, but it wasn't.

Life was like a nightmare for me. I had several great-aunts and some great-uncles living in the same house. I thought life was going to be better, and I could go to school, have clothes, and other nice things. Instead, what I found was that the life they lived was not the kind of life I wanted.

My great-aunts and great-uncles lived a life full of gambling and drinking from the time they woke up in the morning until bedtime and would start over again the next day. My time was spent taking care of them, and there was no time for school.

By then, I was in the 7th grade and barely knew what to do. So I decided to go back home and go back to school. After school, I went to work at the home of a white schoolteacher until 10:00 p.m. When I got home, I had to do more work.

In 10th grade, I dropped out of school again. This is when my dad moved out of our house for good.

I continued to work outside of the home. When I was told I had to go work in the sugar cane fields, I decided to go back to school and stay in school the rest of my life. I was not going to let the blades of those sugar canes cut my legs.

I worked every day and never kept any of my money because my mother needed it. I didn't have any shoes when it was time to go back to school, and I had hand-me-down clothes. I went to my grandmother and explained that I was going back to school and needed shoes. She gave me a $1.00 and I bought a pair of black canvas tennis shoes. I went back to school in the 10th grade and found room in my work schedule to be a cheerleader and play basketball. Most of the time I warmed the seats, but I was proud to be on the team. My mother was proud that I was doing great in school, participating in plays, and I was determined to do better. I even ran for homecoming queen one year. I did not win, but I was a queen anyway. I was in the court and rode in the Dairy Day Parade on a float. Until this day, my aunt who is three months older than I am still tells that story.

As a teen, I paid attention to store clerks who were not too much older than I was, and I wanted to do this kind of work. I also noticed people working in office positions and decided that was my next job.

I started out as a civil rights fighter at sixteen years old. Although I applied for those jobs, I was not hired until I went to New Orleans to live.

In my junior year of high school, my mother moved to New Orleans after one of my brothers broke his leg and had to have a pin put in it. My mother's family lived in New Orleans at the time. She lived there for several years before becoming ill, and I joined her to help take care of my younger siblings. I did not have a coat even though it was December and cold.

My step-father had a coat and clothes for me to wear when I arrived.

I started working my first dream job as a sales clerk and cashier while I was in 11th grade. My job was at the Ben Franklin 5 & 10¢ Store, where I became the head cashier. I started my first secretarial job at age 19 and worked at the Greyhound Bus Station. From there, the positions just got better.

I learned to keep some of my money every payday so I could pay for my school budget, prom, and my ring. I decided to keep 25¢ out of my pay every payday. I also learned how to save all of my change. Every silver dime was saved and I paid for my own ring and senior budget with dimes.

At the age of 23, I co-signed a loan for my mother and step-dad's first home. I had AAA credit.

I had some health challenges throughout my life from the time I was 13 years old and never gave up. A half of semester into college, I got ill and had to drop out. However, on the LSU Campus is where I found my purpose in life. I had no help on that campus because in 1967 Blacks were not allowed to attend most of the all-white colleges. I never stopped learning and teaching others and directing others on how to overcome circumstances in life. I made sure that I kept up with the job trends and education requirements needed for various jobs and directed others in their career paths.

I could not have done it without FAITH and putting GOD FIRST IN MY LIFE.

MANY TIMES, I DIDN'T KNOW WHAT TO DO. I OWE ALL OF IT TO HIM.

Education is essential to overcome tribulation, along with a mindset of not staying in the same situation from day to day or year after year. It is important to have a positive attitude in all things, find what makes you happy, and especially discern what YOUR GOD GIVEN PURPOSE is.

Prophetess Wanakee M. Brown-Belin

My name is Wanakee, which means "the peaceful one." My name is Cherokee in origin. I am peaceful in life, but I'm forceful, unstoppable, relentless, and sure-footed when it comes to taking care of myself. I have a very different poverty story; it will change your life along with your mind-set.

Wanakee Marie Brown-Belin, prophetess, graduate of Grace Bible College, communications counselor, licensed and ordained minister, Woman of the Word Ministry

The Smell of Poverty

I am a woman who learned early in life that there are several kinds of poverty. I also learned most people think there is only one kind. Society works to rid its people of the "normal poverty," while others are left to figure out what is happening to them in their lives. They struggle to put a name on what is happening. I struggled with this. The kind of poverty I suffered from is far from the "poverty" society deals with. My story will shift your thinking, as I believe a person can suffer from different kinds of poverty. In this kind of poverty, if a person is not careful, they might lose the very essence of who they are! Loss of essence is a loss of yourself and getting "you" back could be a hard long road.

I remember being very young and wondering how poor people were able to get by. I had a wonderful mother and father who taught my two brothers and me to always thank God for all we had. I thanked Him each day. As I grew and always had material things, there was something missing that only I could figure out (as I came to learn). For my 15th birthday, I remember my mother giving me a wonderful card with a message something like, "I have raised you to love God and to treat people with respect no matter what, and you are just as good as and if not better than anyone else in this world." This started a new journey for me, as I found myself loving me but being hated by my so-called friends for having the upbringing that I had. I did not want to be alone in my teen years, but I knew I had to keep myself true to God for loving and protecting me. I really spent more time alone in my life than I spent with people outside of my family. This became dissatisfying to me. My parents worked and provided for us; they wanted us to be "better off" than they were. So I had this wonderful life, but no one that I grew up with wanted to have anything to do with me because of how I grew up. I grew up "people poor"! This affected me in ways that I am just now starting to understand. Although when I was young and experiencing this poverty, I thought it was 100% negative. As I became an adult, I found out just how positive something like this can be. I learned that poverty takes on many shapes and it means different things to different people. No matter what kind of poverty a person is experiencing, it hurts!! I came to understand the meaning of spiritual poverty, the kind I had in my life. I know that judging people can do some serious damage and no one should be judged. My poverty was spiritual and because it was not physical poverty, I was almost judged beyond recognition. So I had to pick myself up and truly learn how to love me! I loved me so much that no one can ever penetrate the armor of my self-love.

I also learned that when a person shows self-love, it is sometimes not received well by others. I now know the true power of the human language and I use it to bring change on a consistent basis for my life and the lives of others. I know that positive speaking and positive thoughts are a form of love! Throughout my life I have assumed the burden and reached out to people who seemed to be unreachable. Some people don't have the level of love that they desire in their lives, and in looking for it, all kinds of emotions surface on a daily basis. I am a communications counselor who teaches and counsels on the effects of speaking properly and positively. My internal self-talk saved me as a teenager. I now understand and resolve that it does not matter if I am all alone in this world because I know God is always with me and He will never leave me! God is my mother, my father, my brothers, all aunts and uncles and every family member that I could ever have! Now with this being said, when God sends people into my life, I count it all joy! And I take the relationship for what it is. Because as sure as the sun rises each day, people will come and people will go from my life, but the Father is always with me. So I enjoy my life and all of the relationships that come my way. Loving, laughing, learning, and teaching, I took a good look around me and I saw just how blessed I am. I am a healthy 60-year-old woman who enjoys a loving relationship with Jesus and my family.

I started to take all of the time necessary to continually work on myself to make my whole life better. My Bible tells me that I have it all in Jesus' name and I always move forward to prove the Bible correct! From great credit to supernatural health, I have it; I bless God for it every morning, noon, and night. The loneliness that I feel now is different. (There is an unhealthy and a healthy loneliness.) I spend time with people who are placed in my life. Most of them are not friends, a word that is overused and misused. Yes, I do have friends. I am thankful for my family and my spiritual daughter. I'm rich in love in my life, and I'm thankful for the people who come my way. There is nothing better than accepting your life and fully enjoying it.

Wanakee,

The peaceful one

<u>Faye Thomas Fulton-Venerable</u>

Licensed minister: Pastor Mack & Brenda Timberlake Christian Faith Center-Bread from Heaven Bible Institute 1985. Ordained pastor: Bishop Leroy & Pastor Lois McKenzie Faith Assembly Christian Center 2000. Anointed and appointed prophet: Apostle Willie J. Sturgess & Pastor Betty Sturgess Full Gospel Deliverance Center 2003, at Divine Destiny Center Trinadad with Apostle Vivian Duncan & Pastor Jemma Duncan 2003. Daughter of Pastor Odessa Venerable & businessmen Thomas Venerable. Education, skilled training, services, and work: A.A.S. in paralegal, B.S.C.J. forensic psychology, M.S.C.J./Law School. One year toward Ph.D. in clinical counseling, psychology community leader, GF Fulton Foundation, business owner of Tryself Computer Learning Center, business owner of P31 IMAGO DEI ENTERPRISES, editor-in-chief P31 VIRTUOUS WOMEN'S MAGAZINE.

As an ordained pastor and prophet, I have been called by God to serve. My primary objective is to teach and preach the word of God, the purpose of the Holy Spirit, the Fruit of the Spirit, and the nine gifts of the Spirit to the body of Christ to those who are young Christians or believers who need to be taught, rooted, and grounded in the word of God. I seek only to do what God has called me to and to serve, seek, and present Christ to a lost and dying world. I ask for fervent prayers to all who took time to read this belief history.

The Smell of Poverty

Coming up I knew very little about poverty. If we were poor, I knew nothing about it. I'm sure my parents were poor while living in the South, but they moved to Long Island, New York, where my father, Thomas Venerable, whom I was named after, became a very prosperous businessman. My mother was in ministry and established two churches, one in New York and the other in North Carolina. My mom and dad had nine children but raised 18 to 19 kids under one roof. My eldest sister passed away at the age of 35, leaving eight kids behind. I was disobedient as a teen. I got pregnant and married at age 17. This is where living in poverty and being poor became my first real encounter. I lived this way, sleeping in parks and vehicles with four kids and my then very young husband. Yes, four kids by the time I was 23. My kids were never stable. I washed them up in McDonald's;

this went on for 13 years. However, my situation then never made me feel poor even though my living conditions were very poverty stricken. Although most days I did not eat, I got through it. In 1989, I finally divorced my then-husband.

More importantly, I really felt poverty in 2017. I was married again and stayed married for 18 years, then separated from him for five years. In the summer of 2017 I was homeless. I had no place to live, ate hash browns for breakfast from McDonald's and, once again, I was bathing in the bathroom. It took me back to those years as a married teenager. It was a sad, very pitiful time in my life, just this past summer. I slept in the heat in a beat-up car. I didn't realize how weather-beaten I was. I felt the weight of poverty like no other time in my life. After a few weeks, I was rescued by a precious relative who took me in for four months. I'm ok now:, God has given me purpose and direction. Do I have it all together? Am I rich? Do I have a house? No to all those questions, but I most certainly do not feel impoverished either. I'm the editor-in-chief of my own magazine called *P31 Virtuous Women's Magazine*, and I'm working on several other businesses. I thank God for people like Shannon. God knew I needed her in my life and I value her strength, courage, patience, and love. I look forward to the next chapter in my life, because at one point I wanted to die and begged God to take me because life was just too painful. Is everything perfect? No, but I'm not where I once was in poverty. Poverty, like I said, wasn't something I knew or grew up in. I think poverty comes in many forms. But, lacking the necessities of life and struggling to eat, with no home, no income, and no transportation are all poverty to me. You see, I was raised in a generation and within my community where the man took care of the wife. I wasn't raised to understand women's "lib" or women's independence. Yes, my mom was in full-time ministry, but that was her calling. Her first call was to be a wife, mother, and homemaker. This was all I knew and understood and it was a mind-set and culture for me. I married with those thoughts in mind. However, the day came when my husband left. I realized then how much I depended on him for everything. I was scared, frightened, confused, and wondering what to do at the time. It wasn't like I never worked before, but I was crippled in knowing how to fully take control of life. It's hard to explain really. I'm sure today's women would say, "REALLY?" I've recovered from a very painful divorce and broken family relationships. My story is not unique, but uniquely experienced by me. So, how did I come out? I surely almost didn't make it. I almost died in my situation. But God, for his grace and mercy, brought me through it. I came out by His love. I came out because I had to find strength in Him to overcome. The few relatives who took me in gave me a place of refuge, a place to rest, and recover. I'm much better now, not fully all together, but better. I'm project oriented. I use creativity to fight back depression, hurt, pain, and disappointments. I create something that makes me smile and feel good inside and I pray. I seek God's face for direction. I came out by finding something to call my own. Whether it's a success or not, it's mine and I can give it life, or I can kill it. It's my decision. You see, my problem is that I'm too real, too open, too giving, and so I get hurt. Despite it all, I have learned to forgive no matter what befalls me. What does this have to do with poverty? Everything! Life can throw any of us into a situation where we find ourselves out on the street, right where I once was. There's a whole lot more to this story you wouldn't even think possible or believe. The smell of poverty is just that: it's an odor of a certain way of living that can strike out of nowhere, but a way of life for many. I was fortunate enough to have a father who didn't allow any of his children to smell, think, or feel the weight of poverty. I stepped out into life unprepared at a very young age with no life skills, and poverty seemed like it became my best friend. From 17 until now it's been a struggle. But God is good and has allowed me to overcome a mind-set of poverty. We can find ourselves in poverty due to mistakes we made. I made mistakes in raising kids, mistakes in marriage, mistakes in work, and mistakes in business. Poor judgment in various areas of life led me to poverty. I ask forgiveness from family, and a few friends, if my poor judgment or mistakes in life caused you any pains. Please forgive me now. I forgave myself, and I want to do well and make life soar. I want to leave a legacy to my grandchildren of peace, love, and prosperity for their future. It's not about me anymore; it's about the future of them. Some things can't be helped when experiencing poverty; it was about survival and maintaining until I could do better. NO EXCUSES, JUST BEING REAL!

<u>Shannon Griffin</u>

As a child and adult in poverty, Shannon understands the struggle, the pain, and the humiliation of not having the basic essential to live. She has served individuals and her community for over 20 years. As a child on public assistance, we had a social worker who would come to the house to check on her family. Her compassion and caring is what influenced her to become a social worker and help others today.

I've had a wonderful person come into my life and told me to "quit playing small" with my gifts, so here I am.

As a child, you don't understand why you're poor. You don't understand why food is not in your refrigerator when you come home from school. When you move into adulthood, she begins to learn that poverty and education are related. Shannon saw that education is a must have to get you beyond your poverty. This project is design to educate and assist those that want to come out of poverty by being educated by your story.

Continuing in that field of social work, I wanted to give back. Shannon looks forward to you being a part of the project and changing the Smell of Poverty.

Oh Lord, What's that Smell?

One would stop and wonder why life was so hard and why did others have opportunities availed to them that I didn't. As a young child born into poverty, I could only imagine asking such a question—what's that smell. Could it have been that I was one of six in a home of fatherless children? Could it have been that I was born from a single mother caring a mixed bag fleeing from generations of poverty, secrets, and shame? I would have to ask the question of "How did this happen?" and "Am I in the right place?" These questions could have only been in my imagination and getting answers would be like waiting in a free food line.

Being the youngest of six and one of three girls was how my life started in Oakland. In 1968, I was born into poverty as the child of two adults from different eras, but coming together all the same. Being conceived without my permission to be a part of this life was the decision of God and only He knew what was planned for me. My mother was from the deep south of Arkansas, and she met my father on her travels from Arkansas to Seattle then to California.

In the late 60s, Oakland was a city where poverty was the norm and where civil activism and opportunity ran rampant in the street. Oakland, California (aka "The Town"), was where high levels of poverty and police brutality set the scene, and Huey P. Newton was the neighborhood recruiter. This is where free breakfasts were handed out everywhere and it was the lifeline for most folks in the neighborhood. It was a city filled with poverty, prosperity, and oak trees. We grew up in a place where the local pool hall was our playground and the local park was the daycare center.

Living in west Oakland was where we spent many years around a generation of adults who were born in the 40s and 50s and didn't give a damn about conforming to the rules. They had seen a revolution and wanted to enjoy life despite having children. We lived in poverty but didn't realize it until we'd go to the refrigerator to get food and found nothing was there. Poverty was a way of life, but on the 1st and the 15th of the month, we got our life back because it would look like the entire grocery store left an abundance of food for us to eat. During this time, it was like Christmas twice a month. If you could only see the smiles on our faces when food would come into the house, you would know it was one of the happiest moments of our life. When the light would get cut off because my mother didn't have the money to pay the bill, we got plenty of rest. Since there was no television to watch, we spent long days outside and went to bed early. You could say that at the time, this was an awful situation to have to live with as a child, and I would have to agree with you. However, when I think about how television distorts our reality, I think I'm good. We lived in a housing authority building, so on days when food was gone, we were resourceful. We would go to a friend's house and eat, or we would crowd the local Carnation's milk truck for milk and ice cream. We were resourceful, so picking lemons from the local neighborhood trees to sell lemonade was a natural instinct to get money to buy food.

On many of the days when we didn't have food in the house, my brother made sugar cookies from scratch. They were golden brown and shaped like kidneys and were the best sugar cookies I had ever eaten. Looking good was not important to six kids surviving poverty, but the taste was great and we weren't hungry that night. Not knowing the impact of poverty on our lives or what poverty really meant, my brothers, sisters, and I knew survival was a must, and "waste not" were the gospels. Oh Lord, what's that smell? I knew I didn't want to live in poverty anymore, and I knew there would be a way to escape its generational hold, and I would find a way to get what society has and do what I could to see better days.

As a child on public assistance, we had a social worker who would come to the house to check on us. Back then, welfare works would come to the house for home visits. I know our worker saw we weren't living so cool. I remember feeling as though we were being visited by the police because we had to hide the color TV in the closet. If the worker saw what was considered a luxury or expensive things in your home like a color TV, you could lose welfare assistance and that would not be cool. Our worker had compassion for us because one day she took us to the circus. Her compassion made an impact on my life because I wanted to be a social worker and do things to bring smiles, hope, and opportunity to a child in poverty.

In the modern world, POVERTY is the lack of necessities that keep you alive and moving in this world. Without these necessities, like food, money, and shelter, life is difficult. Nevertheless, I didn't say impossible because mindset is the necessity that will get you off your butt to move something and climb your way out of a poverty situation.

Now don't get it twisted about this smell of poverty, which is real and still lurks in the walls of my subconscious thoughts. When I least expected it, I said, "Oh Lord, what's that smell"; the whole house was reeking of poverty. When I understood that in order to rid this smell from my subconscious mind, I would have to get educated and be in a position that would feed me, and provide housing and my necessities. A little black girl who was once on welfare, holding onto food and shelter, and a high school dropout turned two degrees and street knowledge into a life filled with love, compassion, who provides other necessities to friends and family. I'm not where I was, but I know God has more for me. As I share this with you, I can still smell POVERTY.

Adrianne Johnson

Adrianne Johnson is the founder of ReBuilt, which is a company dedicated to teaching caregivers of at-risk girls how to develop meaningful relationships while utilizing the eight dimensions of wellness. Miss Johnson lives in Pensacola, Florida, and serves as a children's case manager at Lakeview Center. Miss Johnson has spent over a decade advocating, mentoring, and teaching at-risk youth in her community while serving in several different capacities.

The Smell of Poverty

I was in dire straits trying to get to Mobile, Alabama that Thursday night. The concert had started at 7:00 pm and the current time was 7:40 pm. That evening, my church obligations could not be overlooked. My niece, Fantasia, offered to ride with me to Mobile. She had a homework assignment to complete; however, she stated that she would type it on my laptop while I drove to the University of South Alabama.

As I drove onward from Pensacola, Florida, into the state of Alabama, I was anticipating seeing the city lights of Mobile. Fantasia was feverishly typing on the laptop. After a quick glance, I saw that she was working on a PowerPoint presentation and inquired why. She laughed and explained it was a homework assignment. I could see a sign indicating the Battle Park Bridge was ahead so I merged onto the bridge as my 17-year-old niece told me a story.

She said, "You know when I was a little kid, my mom would take my brothers, sisters, and me to Mobile. Mom had a boyfriend who lived in Mobile and every day for like six months or so we went to Mobile to see him. She would pick us up from school and we would head there. Sometimes I would be so tired and sleepy, but I couldn't sleep. The bottom of the car floor had holes in it and I was afraid to go to sleep."

As I gripped the steering wheel, my mind wandered back to when I met Fantasia when she was 11 years old. Over the years, I had seen her endure some difficult situations; however, I never heard her talk about them. Fantasia became a member of my family through reaching out to my sister, Andrea, at church during a Bible study session. It was their first encounter. My sister was 21 years old when Fantasia boldly asked Andrea to be her godmother. Andrea was hesitant at first; however, she could tell by the child's appearance she needed a little assistance.

After spending time with Fantasia, Andrea discovered she was a youth who had been diagnosed with leukemia at the age four. Fantasia's family living situations always appeared unstable during the first few months of their new blossoming relationship. One day my sister told me she had a goddaughter. I was happy for her. Andrea looked elated and told me she would bring Fantasia to my apartment later that day. I thought she was a toddler. Little did I know, my sister had a tall, gangly pre-teen under her charge. The first time I met the wide-eyed youth, she struggled to make eye contact, and spoke with a voice that strained to speak clearly. It was apparent that she tried to please my sister in everything she did; however, unbeknownst to

Fantasia, she had found a reliable resource in my sister.

Within my first year of knowing Fantasia, her family had moved several times in the city of Pensacola. There were times Fantasia would be at my sister's place for weeks at a time. Andrea made room in her living space for the child's belongings. I became very familiar with this awkward child, and it was very rare for me to see Andrea without seeing Fantasia with her. My sister began to teach her about personal hygiene. At this time, Fantasia was linked to different other vital adults whom my sister was associated with.

Fantasia was assisted by a woman who had access to discount clothing and it was much needed. Over time, I realized that Fantasia's situation at home was severely unstable and did not appear to improve. At times, it seemed to get worst and looked bleak. Eventually, I saw

Fantasia's living situation with my sister looked to be a permanent situation. About two years after meeting Fantasia, my sister and I rented a nice apartment together closer to the University of West Florida. We both were students there.

At this time, Fantasia was in the 8th grade and it was apparent that the time invested in her was meant to evoke true lasting results for a life of being self-sufficient. It was in the best interest of Fantasia to transfer her to another school the following year to establish an appropriate foundation for entrance into college. It was already in the heart and mind of Fantasia's godmother that the young teenager would attend college for legal studies. During this time, I encouraged Fantasia to read more. I was relentless at times. During her leisure time of watching television, I suggested that she select the "closed-caption" option. This would allow her to see unfamiliar words she heard during the program. Fantasia was also encouraged to write book reports to enhance her way of thinking. While we had plans for Fantasia's future, her mother was unsure if her daughter could actually be successful at a mainstream public school. After several discussions, Fantasia's mother conceded and allowed her to attend public school.

Fantasia struggled her first semester in high school. The school required more of her academically. She spent several hours each night doing remedial coursework assignments. At the charter school she had previously attended, Fantasia excelled in her academics. Depending on Andrea's work schedule, she would assist Fantasia with assignments. If Andrea worked second shift (from the hours of 3–11 pm), she would review her assignments once she came home. Sometimes the two would stay up unto the wee hours of the morning working on mathematics. Since mathematics was never my strong suit, I assisted with the other subjects as needed. By the end of the semester, Fantasia was progressing and our family had acquired another teenager, Tyrius Savage. Ty was a rambunctious, soulful singing 18 year old who aged out of foster care but was not ready to be out on his own. He attended church with us and was under my brother's mentorship. Ty attended school with Fantasia and was very protective of her.

I was reminiscing about all that Fantasia had overcome since I had known her as I pulled up to our destination. We scurried in the cold winter night to the University of South Alabama Amphitheater. As we approached an usher for the event, we were told the concert was ending and they were not allowing anyone access to the facility. I looked at Fantasia, my high school senior, and we decided to take pictures. We hurried back to the car with the same excitement as we had when we departed the vehicle. We went to a local eatery before heading back to Pensacola. Despite missing the concert, I really enjoyed myself with Fantasia. As we were crossing the Battle Ship Parkway Bridge, I said something to Fantasia, but she did not respond. I looked over to her and my teenage girl was asleep. I sighed deeply as tears welled up in my eyes and my car left that bridge. I exhaled and said, "You are safe, you are loved, and I'm taking you home."

Dee Marie Jones

As a former bride herself, Dee Marie knows the stress that comes with planning that "Big Day Event." When all a bride wants to do is enjoy the thought of marriage, Dee Marie was stressing over organizing and planning her event, being drilled about the wedding details by friends and family, and running around looking for that special place to hold her big day. Could you imaging the stress that would bring to a bride? "No bride should have to think about all these things when trying to enjoy the thought of getting married in the first place." For the past nine years, Dee Marie has been planning events from corporate to bridal events. Brides hire her to help move them from overwhelmed to organized and planning their own dream wedding.

Going Back to Step Forward

I recently came to learn of my great-grandfather, Levi Maguire, who came to be an indigent slave at the age of 16 and would not become a freeman until the age of 21. You see, my Grandpa Levi and his parents were enroute to return to Africa in early to mid-1800. Unfortunately, my great-great-grandparents ran out of money once they finally reached New York. They were enslaved and separated from their son, my Grandpa Levi. It was then that my Grandpa Levi was placed into slavery to earn what was already given to us by Our Heavenly Father, and that was the right to live and be free. Once free, Grandpa Levi would meet my great-grandmother, Maggie, and they married and raised six children.

Grandmother Mary was one of Grandpa Levi's six children who was on my mother's side of the family. Although Grandmother Mary is now deceased, she is very much alive in my mind, heart, and soul. Fortunately, the world can see my grandmother's work in the attached news article regarding her diligence in and around the community while living in San Francisco, California. It was amazing for me to see and learn of the community my grandmother built around her. I may never do all that my grandmother did, but the lesson is obvious and she had a team!

My Grandma Mary loved all of her grandchildren dearly and showed it freely. Grandma Mary also loved the San Francisco 49ers, which permeated on down to many of us to this day. You will notice in my Grandma Mary's news article, that it does not tell anything about the things she enjoyed or pieces of her personality, hobbies, or gifts and talents. The article tells what she cared about and what her passions. However, what I know about my

Grandma Mary, I know from being in the room with her speaking cornbread to us about life. I learned how to cook and bake by spending time in the kitchen with her. I know my great-grandpa Levi and my great-grandma Maggie because I spend time with my mother who gives me the inside scoop of who they were from what my grandma Mary told her. So my point is, we have heritage. By taking time to go around the corner, in some cases, to see your grandparents and older ones in your family, you, too, will learn. You will grow in your confidence and self-development as you learn and see from the people who paved the way for you and your own family. It has been an amazing journey to go back. It has helped me see more clearly how to go forward in my own pursuits, for survival, and in the interest of my own children. Because I spent time with the older ones in my family, I have only scratched the surface and I will keep going back as far as I can. I want to know my paternal and maternal heritages to the best of my ability, but my true heritage is that of a spiritual one. The lineage of David that Jesus Christ came through is more important than heritage in the larger scheme of things. Once I was able to prioritize that part, my fingers could flow more freely over my keyboard and I was able to enjoy the freedom. My great-grandpa Levi was enslaved to regain not only the freedom he once had before he was separated from his parents, but he had to regain the freedom that Our Heavenly Father already bestowed on us as a blessing. I'm sure my grandfather Levi had to work on his mindset because once free, the U.S. Census does not reveal him working for anyone but himself. He must have maintained a confidence that would be his reality once free again, and he and his wife and most of their children as they worked at their own business owners in their own right.

One of things I want you to get from my story is the understanding that even though we have the benefit of Ancestory.com and the U.S. Census reports, it cannot be overstated that time spent getting to know your family heritage is invaluable. Our family heritage can give some insight to who we are. I want my children to understand and always know the value of spending time with family. It provides some of life's greatest lessons and knowledge that has the power to enrich our life and lift us up as we take on our own life's journey as a gift from Our Creator.

I know my grandma Mary was an excellent cook, baker, and even a candy maker. She loved family and reading. My grandmother was also a seamstress and she made my mother's clothes. My mother's winter coat, crafted by my grandmother's hands, and other youthful clothing in her pictures were always so stylish. My mother's style is a reflection of my grandmother, and I cherish that legacy from both of them both. My mother has beautifully designed swimsuits, so don't be surprised if you see Maggie Swims in a store near you someday soon! I mention these things simply to underscore the importance of sitting with the older ones in your family. While newspaper articles of one's secular achievements are nice, there is nothing better than being able to make your grandmother's famous family gumbo or realize that you have the ability to create a business like my great-grandpa Levi and his parents did. You see, my great-grandpa Levi and his parents did not taste slavery in New Jersey. They worked and owned businesses and later owned property once Grandpa Levi was a freeman and later married my great-grandma

Maggie. The U.S. Census from 1887 – 1910 shows my great-grandparents earned wages in their own businesses and did not have a poverty mindset. I would imagine that in those times, running a successful business was not easy by any stretch of the imagination. I take that and I carry it with me as a reminder, that even though I have my struggles, knowing where I come from has truly helped me. First, I have written these words myself; but more importantly, it has made me feel more complete in my being. It has answered questions I have about my own dreams, hopes, and desires, where come from, and that I have the drive to pursue what I want. Entrepreneurship is in my blood. My people did not succumb to a poverty mindset. I do not come from that stock. Somewhere along the way I was lied to; and what is worse, I believed the lie! The lie told me that corporate America was my dream. That was not my dream! I would have never set myself up behind cubicle walls, which block the view from my window in a dreary two-story office building. Nor would I have dreamed of raising my family while struggling just over broke and believe that I'm winning! I am incensed that I fell for the okey doke, the hoodwink, was led astray and ran amok. That would have never been what I would have naturally chosen for myself and surely not for my children and my children's children! I'm incensed, I am determined, to continue to overturn that stench, that awful smell of a broken mindset, and rebuke the smell of poverty from my midst. You may ask well why now, and all I can say to that is, why not. I came across ten affirmations that have helped me daily as I move from the indigent slave to a freewoman just as my legacy taught me to do so I too may pass on a freedom to my children and my children's children. I want them to know, understand, and have faith that Our Creator did not make us to sit in cubicles and rot away in misery to provide for our families. However, if that is what one chooses, then there is no shame in it. What I want my family to know and understand is that their faith will give them the power and knowledge to know that there are other options. Those options exist in their own hands, in their own gifts, and in their own talents. Should they so have the desire, they will be able to pursue their dreams if they work hard to achieve them. I want my family to know their heritage and where and whom they come from because I refuse to let my kids be hoodwinked, led astray, and run amok. I want my family to see themselves as my great-grandpa Levi, a businessman, and their grandma Maggie who also came from a family of business owners and homeowners. So as the article can only describe my grandma Mary in the way of her accomplishments. It will never tell you who my grandma really was from my youthful standpoint. A community leader, activist, and lover of her community are clearly seen in this news clip that I am honored to have my hands on. I say that because we often lose family heritage and the intimate history of our ancestors as close as a grandmother or grandfather simply because families do not get around to documenting their life's experiences and accomplishments. There was no question about including my grandmother's work in my story. My grandmother on my father's side was an excellent cook as well and originally came from Louisiana. I inherited her gumbo recipe and ran with it. I will keep running with it as her only legacy to me. However, her love and influence as a strong Black woman will always be with me. I love my family dearly and am thankful for the gems they passed down to us as children. It is my wish that when my family reads these words, they continue to take time to look into our family heritage as well as the spiritual heritage we have available to us.

Elizabeth KorKor

Elizabeth KorKor was one of 10 children born in harsh living environments and mothered in a climate with high infant mortality. Living is harsh with a living environment struggling with the crucial epidemic of poverty. Elizabeth was born to farmers. Elizabeth was not educated through modern privileges of schools, but she learned by working the fields and harvesting what was grown on the land. Giving life to 12 kids on the land of what is the birthplace of slavery, Elizabeth has seen much to be desired of her people snatched from their homeland and held in the clutches of colonizers never to see their homes, families, or life as they knew it again. Elizabeth is said to be 120 years old and looks to share her life's story through storytelling as what has been cultivated by Ghanaian people passed on throughout the generations.

The Smell of Poverty

The Smell of Poverty has been said to smell like extreme poor hygiene, poorly insulated houses coupled with leaky walls and bathrooms. Poverty in general is musk of disrepair, perhaps a result of mildew and old garbage that has sat in the house so long that flies have laid eggs in there and maggots have hatched. You don't want to take that trash out again because you just placed a new plastic bag in the can and the trashcan is not full yet. It's kind of hard to get that smell out without a seriously good cleaning cycle; however, without the money dedicated to buy the cleaning products, the smell of poverty is there regardless of social class/work ethic.

Although quite a few of the poor I've known have simply had really raw deals in life (born poor, bad families, quit school to work to feed themselves and families, discrimination, and slavery), I have noticed that many poor people carry the odor that I have often thought of as.....

Personally, I've never seen extreme third-world poverty, and some of the causes of that smell of poverty are different. Some would say that American poor typically have only themselves to blame for their predicament. Regardless of how one feels about poverty and whose fault it is, most of the people living in poverty in this country are children. My heart is broken when I see children who are living in these conditions and going hungry.

This brings me to a story of poverty about a woman I've come to know as "Theresa's Grandma." Her poverty story is a narrative because Theresa's grandma lives in Greater Accra, Ga Ghana and she doesn't speak English.

I was not fortunate to have a live interview with her; nevertheless, I was honored to meet Theresa through Facebook. I learned of her grandmother's story of poverty. Theresa estimates that her grandma, Elizabeth KorKor, was born in 1898. Family members can't remember the exact month, but based on farming seasons, it may have been in the month of February, March, or June. Her birth certificate was not available to confirm because birthdays are not celebrated in Africa. Elizabeth has a younger sibling who is still living at the age of 97 and she has relatives who estimated her age at 120 years old. Since neither of my parents were thought about 120 years ago, I will use this as confirmation and my reference point in time.

Elizabeth was one of 10 children with five sisters and four brothers; unfortunately, some of her siblings died before Elizabeth was born. Infant mortality was all around because of the harsh living environment and crucial epidemic of poverty. Elizabeth was born to farmers who grew peanuts, tomatoes, okra, and peppers.

Elizabeth wasn't book educated, but was a wealth of knowledge, nonetheless. Going to school was not one of life's pleasures or pains that she was able to experience because she had to work the land to feed her family and take them to the market to sell and trade. Unlike modern day currency that we use, Elizabeth and her family used seashells to buy what they needed to survive. The shells were a commodity that held high value like currency.

Elizabeth birthed 12 kids, but four of her children died because of no food to eat. Infant mortality was high because the harsh living environment and crucial epidemic of poverty. The babies would be strapped on the backs of their mothers and the women would have to walk for three days to her village, but the child would survive the sweltering heat and starvation. Ghanaian people celebrate a festival called the Homowo, which literally means "hooting at hunger." The celebration takes place in August for the people to remember the great famine that hit the country hard during the sixteenth century. It is also a time for males to have their rights of passage, and they would re-enact historic war events outfitted in traditional battle dress.

These traditions and rituals are from the strong Ashanti people, but this picturesque thought of triumph and celebration has also been scorned with despair. It began with the slave trade when the British set foot on Ghanaian land, violently seeking to capture and extract men, women, and children. It changed the very existence of African people in Ghana and abroad as they were forced into slavery. When Elizabeth was a child and the British came, she and her people ran deep into the forest to areas not easily accessible for travel. They hid to escape being captured and taken to the castle erected to hold slaves and trade the people of Ghana. Today this fortress is known as El Mina's Castle, a place where men were separated from their families. "The room of no return" was what Ghanaians called it. Elizabeth and her family lived three days by foot, and four hours by car away from El Mina's Castle. Multiple unfortunate, captured people were held in cells where peeing, pooping, and eating all took place in the same spot. The dead would be left to rot among the living. Women who refused to have sex with white soldiers were stripped of their clothes and chained to cannons by their hands and legs. This was the last memory of those who were captured, kidnapped from their homeland, and shipped across the Atlantic never to see their families again. A large part of the history of the Ghanaian people was passed along by storytelling, so as I share this story with you we are continuing their history and legacy of a true ancestor who is with us today.

William T. Matthews, O.D.

William Matthews, O.D., is a therapeutic optometrist licensed in the states of Texas and Georgia. A native Texan, William attended the historic Huston-Tillotson University, located in

Austin, Texas, where he majored in biology and mathematics. He obtained his graduate degree from the University of Houston with a doctorate of optometry in 2013.

Licensed in both the states of Texas and Georgia, William has the honor of working closely with patients, and they often open their hearts and express some of their most intimate feelings and deepest concerns. He believes a major facet to health is a peace of mind, so providing comfort and quality of care is essential to William. Advocating for student advancement in higher education is one of his passions. He enjoys traveling for work. He most definitely enjoys traveling domestically and internationally for leisure and clarity of the mind. Staying grounded while on the go for William is something that can be challenging but is possible. The world is global and William is eager to be a part of its progressive direction.

THE SMELL OF POVERTY

You ever have a dream where you are trying to flee, but just cannot seem to get the coordination to run?

I remember the words of my mother, "Chile, you may not remember, but we were poor.

"You were a baby, we lived on base. While your daddy was at work, I would take you on my hip and walk to the grocery store."

The grocery store was off the military base, but adjacent to the military housing where we resided. This was pre 9-11 so entering and leaving the base was with ease. Both of my parents were from Clearwater Beach, Florida, a tourist city across the bay from Tampa. After joining the military, my father was stationed in Fort Hood, the place where I was born and raised.

My mother continued with, "Your tale ate liver a-many-of-nights. I would chew it and give it to you. You don't know what you are missing."

Needless to say, I was grossed out. My mother was not cooking anything special for me on that night. I resented that particular fact, choosing not to have any parts of liver, and attempted to block those words and the thought of the experience from my mind.

All of which was resulting from my not wanting to eat liver on a particular night. My mother, who enjoyed the dish and other meals from Florida, would often mention her childhood experiences including what my great-grandmother would cook. My family relocated from the military base when I was in pre-kindergarten. The three of us moved into the modest, four-bedroom home my parents purchased. This was symbolic for my deliverance from liver.

As if you are stuck in position and striving to become free.

Such an amazing time it was, full of accomplishments and such a time of a lack of self.

Here it is, I became an actual doctor, empathetic to the world of people around me and yet hollow on the inside.

One would ask, how could such a thing be possible? This does not happen overnight,

I started to limit myself. I lacked in making the adequate and functional choices, which billowed into the lack of opportunity for myself and my career. I lacked hope. What a dark place. To be inside of a hopeless space is essentially a prison of the mind. Fear, yes, that thing called fear. Fear plagued me; it was a root and it reared its multiplicity of heads. I had to conquer the fear of the unknown, the fear of change, and the fear of failure.

The voice within me, my subconscious, had committed a coup and was feeding my conscious self-negative thoughts. I no longer saw a white wall in the home as structure,

I saw it as a reason for it to fall and the house to come down with it. The purpose was no longer important; it was the idea of its destruction that was looming in the forefront. I have always been the person who looks at the ramifications of any opportunity or project, but now I am letting those thoughts hold me captive as opposed to finding the "work-around," the solution, the resolve.

Awakened by panic, to realize it was merely a dream.

I am a firm believer that you are your biggest advocate, yet in the moment of shadows, I looked to those around me for comfort, nurturing, and reset. I looked for familiarity, when in actuality, I needed to step into the land of the unfamiliar where the unknowns were not clear.

You look around, and those who are closest to you have stepped aside, because they also have their own river(s) to tread. One would say, "I think that you depend on people too much." And another said, "Twelvy, you have to take actionable steps." Both were a reflection. Both made meaningful impact and were what I had once known myself to be.

I had to tread upstream through those very waters that caressed and allowed me to sail with ease to a point of uncertainty, anguish, and fear.

You begin to realize this is everything but a dream.

Prayer and thoughts, prayer and thoughts. What is prayer worth without recognizing the Exodus? There was a glimmer of hope. I had the key to unlocking the inner turmoil and letting ablaze the fire that burned from within. As with driving a car, there was a brake pedal and it became necessary to apply pressure and take ahold of the steering wheel.

There were things that had to happen in order to progress. I had to step into my light. I had to look at myself. I had to fully embrace all aspects of my past.

I can honestly say, I may have come from poverty, without recognizing the true identity of what poverty represents. But I possessed an impoverished mentality that began to take ahold of my thoughts and actions. There is hope no matter where you are in a situation.

Do not run any longer! Turn around! What are you running from? What you find yourself running from — you often run right into. Understand, the truth will release you from many captives, both psychologically and physically. Love yourself unconditionally and embrace all aspects of yourself, including the flaws. Face the inner beast head on. Whether it is denial, anger, esteem, hurt, betrayal, no matter what your foe may be, look that motherf**ker square in the eye. All of the necessary armor and strength for combat in regaining your life's purpose exists within yourself. Like the phoenix, out of the ashes emerges new beginnings.

When confronting the inner beast, be bold and clear when saying, "I am in control. I got this."

After all, there is nothing to lose, yet everything to gain.

"I'll tell you what freedom is to me. No Fear." ~ *Nina Simone*

<u>Sue May</u>

Cedrick and Sue May have been happily married for 22 years. They are both veterans and have two adult sons. They are the owners of Self Inspired Apparel LLC, an online apparel and accessories company in Northern California. Their focus is to design positive, inspiring, comfortable, quality tees and accessories that emphasize a spirit of self-love and pride. They donate a portion of their proceeds to several nonprofit organizations committed to improving the lives of children and families.

The Smell of Poverty

Ever since my sons were little boys, I have always wanted to design and sell graphic tee-shirts for children. I did not like the shirts in my local department stores because most of them had skulls, snakes, and what I felt were inappropriate sayings. I spent many weekends talking with the store managers about the fashion trends. I was very curious about how to get products into their stores. After visiting many stores, I decided I could design my own tee-shirts for boys. I researched how to register a business and searched for a graphic designer.

I met a graphic designer through a church meeting. She gave me her business card, and I made several attempts to phone and email her. This should have been a hint to me to consider someone else, but my poverty mindset said she was a Christian and God would work it out so she would work with my lack of money and design knowledge. I felt once we met, she would be able to take all the ideas I had been writing down and hopefully make them come to life. I felt God allowed our paths to cross and this was a God-ordained collaboration. After weeks of leaving her messages, with no return calls, she finally phoned me and we scheduled a meeting at a local Starbucks. We drew up a contract and I paid a deposit for a logo design and one business card. She emailed me several potential designs and we settled on one. I met with her to pay the balance and she provided me with a disc and a business card.

I researched local screen-printing companies and identified one. I took the disc to them feeling excited to start producing my children's clothing line. They gave me a tour of their facility and we discussed some tee-shirt prices and packages. Once we settled on a price, they took my disc to open it so we could get started printing tee-shirts. **The disc would not open!!!** I phoned the graphic designer during my meeting at the printing shop. She never answered the phone, so I left her a voice mail message. I provided the screen printing company with her phone number. They informed me that they tried several times to phone her. I was very hurt and disappointed. I saw her one day at church, but I did not approach her. I decided that God would take care of it. I also saw this as a sign that maybe God did not want me to have a business. It was 11 years before I attempted to start another business.

The very thought of owning a business was very daunting to me. I had never owned anything. I wondered if I could ever be a successful business owner. I was raised with an impoverished mentality of being thrifty, "making do" and watching my pennies. I can remember my parents struggling to make $1 out of 15¢. I've heard the phrase about "making your ends meet." It seemed that "ends" had a hard time "meeting" many days in our home. Now as a business owner of an apparel and accessories company, that poor poverty mindset continues to dominate much of my business decisions.

I have always been concerned that people would judge my products, services and me, based on the prices I placed on them. I try to thoughtfully adjust my prices to match their expectations. I find pricing products to be challenging and a miserable way of operating a business. When someone orders a custom product, I usual discuss everything but the price. There have been times when I have asked a customer what they would like to pay. Price swapping for customers has not helped grow my business in terms of revenue or profits. Once, I was told by a local competitor that I was lowballing everyone in the business.

Lowballing? I didn't even know what lowballing was. I have over-extended myself by driving shirts to customer without charging for shipping and handling. I was told many times by other business owners that I needed to leave my fear of success and "poverty mindset" behind if I expected to be successful.

There are days when I ask God, "Is this business something I can do?" I have many reasons for talking to God about why it should be, or why I should not have an apparel business. In my talks to God I would say, "Lord, I have no business trying to run a company. I have no social media or computer skills." I would tell God, "If this is not Your will, I will stop right now and sell the equipment and cut my losses." You see, designing custom and ready-to-wear apparel is all I think about.

My mission is to provide positive, comfortable, quality, inspirational tees and accessories that emphasize a spirit of self-pride.

In line with this mission, I donate a portion of the proceeds to several nonprofit organizations committed to improving the lives of children.

I enjoy designing graphic apparel and if I had it my way, I would give it away. My husband often asks me, "Is this a business or a hobby?" I am finally starting to listen. I realize I am a work in progress, so I have a team who keeps me on target. I am also starting to incorporate some of the following practical steps:

1. Learn to say, **"NO."** I can do anything, but I can't do everything

2. Start the morning with prayer and meditation.

3. Exercise (most successful people take care of their minds and bodies in order to stay focused).

4. Review my business goals daily.

5. Schedule my day (I break down my day in time slots; for example, order shirts by (9:00 a.m.).

6. I am not a slave to my inbox (I review and answer my emails for two hours).

7. Hire a virtual assistant to manage my social media accounts.

8. I have found an amazing business coach.

9. Lastly, I have solicited assistance of an accountability partner to keep me on task. I tend to be a procrastinator. We are in different industries, which allows me to collaborate my products and services with her.

10. Also, I now reach out to other apparel business owners for advice.

My motto is, "Success is the only option, failure is not!!!" It is my uniquely personal vision to never settle and abandon my passion of creating exceptional apparel. I plan to take more risks by stepping out on faith and searching for ways to expand the business internationally. I have crazy faith. It is my belief that I can do all things through Christ who strengthens me (Phil. 4:13). It is never too late to see your dreams come true, but persistence is essential.

<u>Jacqueline McKeever</u>

I am a divorced mom of three adults. I have spent over 16 years in government nonprofit healthcare. While working full time and raising kids, I obtained an MBA with an accounting minor. It wasn't easy doing it alone. Everyone needs a hand sometimes. So in 2016 I created *Route To Victory,* a nonprofit organization created to help individuals learn to manage their money, reduce debt, and build self-reliance.

My Story

I am the founder and the director of Route To Victory. It is a nonprofit, and through it, I am blessed with the opportunity to help people manage their money, build the career they desire, and build the life of their dreams. Thirty years ago, I would not have imagined my life as it is now, or the things I am planning to venture. My story may not be what you think it should be. Yes, I have a poverty story. Unlike some, although I grew up in the projects, I remember not feeling or noticing we were poor until I was nine years old. "Boom" was the sound that would have been made if my life were a movie; but it wasn't a movie.

Before the Boom

I had lived with my great-grandparents until they got sick and went to a nursing home. I grew up in East Gate Terrace Public Housing Apartments ("the Projects"). Many of the people in the area were living in single parent homes or they were moms who received a welfare check and food stamps. At this time, that was not part of my story. My great-grandparents could have had an apartment or a house in a better area. Originally, this area was not bad because when they moved in it was new. Things changed. My sister and I were living a happy childhood where each week we looked forward to candy and some money from our uncle. I really didn't think we were poor because we had new clothes every season, plenty of food, our own television, and everything we needed. If we asked, we could go on the porch or the yard. What more could a kid ask for? We also got new clothes seasonally and lots of toys each Christmas. My great-grandmother was 74 years old and took care of me from the tender age of five months and my sister was one. That made my great-grandfather 85 years old.

The Boom

I was about nine years old when "boom" my great-grandfather died. My great-grandmother had to deal with grief, my mom moving in, and taking care of two children without my great-grandfather's income. To add to this, one of her checks stopped, and she lost her sight due to cataracts. The cataracts may not sound like a big deal, but during the 80s you were hospitalized to have that surgery. Unfortunately, because she didn't have anyone to watch us, she didn't have the surgery. My great-grandmother tried her best to make ends meet with one check, but it was difficult so she decided to go to the Department of Human Resources to sign up for food stamps. When the stamps came in the mail, she sent my sister and me to the corner store. Before leaving, my great-grandmother told me what they were and how to use them. Because I was nervous about using them, I asked a neighbor who used them for years to show me how to use them. After using the stamps a few times, each time I went back home and look at my great-grandmother's face, I discovered we were poor. I noticed men drinking and gambling around the corner instead of working. I noticed how many people came in the store to make purchases with stamps, and they had no shame about it. I noticed how children were poorly dressed. I noticed how Christmas wasn't as bright because we didn't have as many presents under the tree anymore. I noticed our mom didn't work. I started noticing how our apartment was inspected every month. I heard adults saying, "You know you have to hide any good stuff because they will raise your rent if they think you have any money coming in." I noticed my mother didn't wear the perfume as she once did. It was like I had been dreaming all this time and suddenly woke up. My sister was still asleep. It was funny to me how she didn't seem to notice anything that was going on. I was fully aware. It was then I decided to make my own money, save, and learn how to take care of myself so I wouldn't be a burden on my great-grandmother. I asked her to give me instructions on how to cook chicken. From there, I learned to cook food for my sister and me. I also picked up tips from watching cooking episodes on TV shows. My great-grandmother used to pay to get our hair washed and combed. I learned to care for my sister's hair and my hair to eliminate the expense. I practiced reading so I could read mail to her. Without my family's knowledge, I found creative ways to earn money such as playing look out for kids when they were acting badly, or selling candy at school. One could even say I became cautious and aware of my environment. When I also noticed dangers around me, I often warned my sister to be careful. I was also careful not to buy anything I couldn't hide when a state representative came for an inspection. This is the first time I told of how my childhood ended and my adulthood began. Don't get me wrong, I was still a child who occasionally played with dolls and rode my bike, but not as much as I did before realizing we were poor.

Another Boom

I thought the first boom was bad. The second one was even harder. One week my great-grandmother was sick and got worse, so she went to the hospital. From the hospital, my great-grandmother was taken to a nursing home. For a year, I begged people to take me to see her. It never occurred to me that I could have ridden the bus. I guess I forgot to ask how to ride the bus. Finally, a lady in our neighbor took me to see my great-grandmother and that was the last time until her funeral. Things got even tighter around the apartment without my great-grandmother's income. Not only were we on food stamps, but my mother was responsible for us. She received $164 a month from the social services state fund known as Aid for Dependent Children (AFDC), a welfare check, and $31 bi-weekly for child support. That wasn't enough money to take care of two girls. My uncle would contribute by giving her money to buy us clothes and things, but that was once a year and usually around Christmas. He gave her a little each month based on what he could afford. Like any child, my clothes were getting too small for me. I prayed, and we got handouts from people I know for my sister and me. My sister was much smaller than I was so she could wear her clothes longer. My school candy store business was not earning money for me. I found a job at a snack store in the neighborhood, but my mother made me quit when she found out I was working. She was afraid someone would tell the Social Services office and the rent would increase. I knew I had to leave both the apartment and the neighborhood because there was more in store for me and the life of my future children.

Adulthood Signs of Poverty

My childhood exposure to poverty led me to this point of the story. How did my past poverty as a child affect my adulthood? There are many ways, but I will only share a few. I have a desire to save things and money, I wanted to work to take care of my own children and not depend on welfare, and I developed independence and drive. This drive led me to getting a MBA with a minor in accounting and becoming the founder of the Route to Victory. The sad part of the experience was that it gave me a shell-shocked attitude about having things out in the open. Because we had to hide any possessions of value, as an adult I wouldn't put anything on my walls. I had to figure out what the emotion tied to it was. Then one day I started remembering the inspections and it hit me. So to get over it, I just started randomly buying wall decorations and placing them on the wall. Unfortunately, I bought glass décor, and my two boys broke the nice glass things I bought. But that's another story for another time.

Raquel Neal

For the past 15 years RaQuel has been providing coaching, counseling, and consulting services to children and families who have experienced significant challenges and trauma in their lives. She has supported individuals and families with fostering their resiliency to triumph and overcome seemingly insurmountable obstacles using strength based strategies and techniques. She has also successfully navigated her own personal hurdles bringing unique real life wisdom to her practice.

RaQuel earned her master's degree in social work with an emphasis in social justice from Cal State University, East Bay. In addition to private coaching and consulting, she provides training for social workers new to the field around legislative mandates and the use of evidenced based/best practices. RaQuel currently sits on her local county Fairness Equity Task Team and offers consultation and training for government and nonprofit agencies tailored to meet their unique staffing needs.

Poverty Is a Piece of Mind

Let me first start off by saying that poverty is a belief and a state of mind more than it is lacking money in the bank. Poverty is also an illusion purposely programmed in us for control and domination. If people believe they are poor, more often than not, they will be punked into assuming the weaker position. If others believe you are poor they might pity you, but they will likely not empower you. I held a Poverty Piece of Mind for most of my life. It was modeled and taught me that "You are to survive, not thrive." "You gotta rob Peter to pay Paul." "Money don't grow on trees!" "I ain't got it to give." "I ain't got two nickels to rub together." "I ain't got a pot to piss in or a window to throw it out of." "I'm one check away from being homeless." Much of my community was told these lies and then they regurgitated them to our generation and from us to the next. Consistently being told that you are underprivileged, oppressed, and marginalized can become a self-fulfilling prophecy wherein you begin to believe that prosperity and abundance are limited only to a chosen few. It is not. It is available to us all.

Yet this is how millions of people are by design mentally, emotionally, and generationally subjugated. I can just hear the conversation at the big boy table now, "Just get them to believe they're poor then they will have impoverished thinking, and since we know thoughts are things, poverty will appear to manifest itself all around them." I bet they had a big laugh at hoarding this "secret" from folks who don't know who they really are. Now that's not to say that governments don't create barriers, and I would be remiss not to speak facts and acknowledge Black and brown communities being the categorical target of this distortion and deception. But no weapon formed against me shall prosper. Now while I recognize religion is misused as a weapon for impoverishing us to believe we should give all of our money to the church and suffer. I believe God's will for us is to prosper.

I know that today these are the biggest lies ever told and believed across the globe, and for a long time this was my Piece of Mind. Even when we think we are "woke" or "enlightened" as we tell our children that "they can be anything they want," we subconsciously send limiting belief messages: "I can't afford that." "I just need to win the lotto." "You get rich by saving your money." "I just need to marry a rich man." "I just need to graduate." "I'm in debt." "You gotta hustle." "You gotta work hard." "You gotta pray harder." " I can sleep when I die" "The m.an is keeping us down."

First of all, you cannot sleep when you die. Studies show how vital sleep is to our wealth. Secondly, investing versus saving makes more folks rich than not. Lastly, and most importantly, there is no one keeping you anywhere. However, belief in any lie will become our perceived reality when we give it power through our thought, voice, and action. The first key to unlocking any mental chain is to understand that what we think affects how we feel." What we feel affects what we say. What we say affects what we do. What we do affects what we experience. Hear me when I say this, there is unlimited abundance of wealth and health available to us all. However, to realize this is to know how worthy you are of having it. This is the second key. And not only how worthy you are, but how worthy everyone else is, too. Know that when you hate on someone for whatever reason, the Poverty Piece of Mind is activated, and if you're not mindful enough to deactivate it, then you are sure to be impacted in some shape, form, or fashion. One day an NFL player is making it rain and the next it's raining tax evasion on him.

So regardless of what others are thinking, saying, doing, or not doing, you must know that an abundance of health, wealth, and prosperity is yours for the having and the keeping. I'm not going to pretend that unraveling the delusion of poverty is easier said than done. I will acknowledge that we are bombarded with a ton of noise and more of which we voluntarily entertain to entertain us. Hip Hop and rap are filled with lyrics that uplift bling and bags while shaming their brothers and sisters who ain't got it like they do. If I had a nickel for every time someone on reality TV tried to humiliate another for being "broke," I'd be rich right now. Yes, I have habits. Don't judge me.

What really matters is that today we are being modernly bamboozled into thinking that if your Louis Vuitton is real and mine is a knock off, then somehow that makes you more worthy. We are tricked into buying stuff that makes us look rich when we are really creating wealth for someone else's company. Or, if you went to Howard and I went to San Jose State then you are more valuable. This is exactly the type of white supremacist thinking that aims to impoverish us. Now they just sit back and let us do it to each other. It amazes me to see people believe that if they can afford a Chanel bag or some Gucci shoes, then they have somehow arrived. Here is a news flash: money don't make you rich. You can buy stuff, but it cannot create the type of wealth that truly matters.

There are a lot of miserable people with a lot of money, and a lot of people who do not participate in popping tags but have a priceless Peace of Mind. What most people want, though, is the entire package: alignment with wealth, health, and happiness. What most people don't understand is the power to have it all lies within us, and is ignited by how we feel, not how we floss.

The flow of our thoughts and feelings is akin to a powerful magnet attracting to us a reflection of ourselves. How you feel about any situation will yield to you the realized results, desirable or not. Poverty is only a Piece of Mind that tells us that there is another piece we can access to tell a different story and create a divergent ending. The third key is you must have an unwavering knowing that it can be yours. I'm still recreating my story by unlearning some of the indigent financial behaviors. The beauty in all of this is the only thing that really matters is that I have Peace of Mind, and by virtue of that, will acquire everything I desire.

<u>Julia Royston</u>

Author, publisher, speaker, teacher, and songwriter residing in southern Indiana with her husband, Brian K. Royston. Julia's mission is to "Motivate you to be all that you can be, Help you get your Message to the Masses, Turn your Words into Wealth, and Be a Book Business Boss." She realizes that "People hire her to coach them through the Write, Publish and Promote process of a Book, Create Products and Services and Build a Business surrounding a Book."

Julia has written 50 books, and published and coached 120+ authors to release 150+ books. Prior to full-time publishing and coaching, Julia spent 22 years as a certified, media specialist/technology instructor in a public and private school system.

For more information about Julia and her companies, visit http://www.juliaroyston.net

Poverty Starts to End in Your Mind

I believe that poverty not only has a smell but it has a look, speech, and lifestyle; but more importantly, it has a mindset. To me, the mindset is what really fuels the continuation of poverty in some people's life or the lives of the next generation.

I wasn't raised in poverty. I was raised with the mantras of hard work and education. If you work hard and get a good education, you will succeed. My father was a 27-year veteran retired teacher in the public school system. My mother was a homemaker. They built a successful cleaning business at night. At the height of their company, they had 50 employees. My mother took care of the business in the daytime and managed her own housekeeping service. My younger sisters and I cleaned with her in the summer time and when we were old enough, we helped the business. Because of our schedules, we ate dinner together and after a short nap, we all helped with the cleaning and whatever else was necessary to keep the business going and thriving. It sounds like a wonderful life and it was. But it isn't everybody's reality. Over the past 22 years, I believe that God wanted me to be exposed to another side and part of life.

I believe that He wanted my life to be balanced. He knew that if I were to impact the world as He saw fit, I needed to be exposed to different lifestyles and not just my own. I needed to not only be able to sympathize but empathize with others as well. Could I put myself into someone else's shoes, maybe? When I became exposed, up close, personal, and had daily contact with poverty, it changed my whole life.

Contrary to my own desires, hopes, and dreams, I have spent the past 22 years in education. I don't know how it happened, but if God intends for something, be guaranteed that it will happen. My father told my sisters and me to get a minor in education along with our other educational pursuits and we told him no way. Well, he and the heavenly Father had other plans. I left corporate America in 1996 and came home to be the librarian/technology teacher at an all-girls Catholic high school. Now, I know what you are thinking: a private school, who was impoverished there? There were plenty of students. The school attracted girls from 42 zip codes in the area and they had an outreach program specifically for girls who could not financially afford to be at this school. It was a great opportunity for the girls, and the administrators were looking for a staff of color, and that was me; thus, my exposure to real poverty began. I had a student once tell me, "Ms. Foree (which was my maiden name), I'm just poor white trash." I told her to never say that again because there is power in your words. If you said it, you thought it, and if you think it and say it, you will ultimately do it. I had students who were working long hours at night to make partial payments for their books, uniforms, and any other fees associated with private school. I had a student whose mother was running from a bad boyfriend. They lived in the projects; at times, the student came to school with a horrible smell, no backpack, and totally ungroomed or prepared for the day at school. I asked her what was going on. She told me her story. She eventually went to live with another student and her adoptive parents just to graduate. Those girls worked their butts off. Other girls didn't have any money problems so they helped students in the school who couldn't afford the new prom or homecoming dress, shoes, or the ticket to attend and participate. No girl was left behind or left out who didn't want to be. Over the past 22 years, I have seen those students rise to be walking alongside me in the educational field, become the engineers they said they would be, and move on to grow and live the life they were exposed to at school. Most of those young women took responsibility for their life but were exposed to more; they worked hard and did it. What about the very young?

In 2006, I got married, moved to a different state and changed school districts. I went from an all-girls private high school to a public elementary school. Talk about culture shock. I was a woman with no children, newly married and now weekly I was literally learning how to teach 500 children under the age of 10. High school students are pretty self-sufficient. Those high school girls played volleyball and stood more than six feet tall. I stand 5 foot 2 inches. Now, I am looking down at children 3 feet tall trying to understand, somehow predict their needs as well as teach them about literacy, technology, and life skills. Lord help me. Needless to say, my first year was overwhelming. I was introduced to a new level academically but more importantly, more problems, issues, family make-ups, poverty, young parents, and abuse to the least able to help themselves, children. Don't underestimate little children. They are creative, manipulative, and use everything that they have to their advantage. These babies may not be old enough to hold down a job, but they are working you all of the time. Why? They are trying to survive. My elementary school population has 86–94% (depending on the enrollment) of its students eligible for free and reduced lunch. No student pays for breakfast, lunch, field trips and may be eligible for clothing, backpacks or food after school. When more than 90% of your population is financially unable to pay for breakfast and lunch that is everybody and not a particular race. Poverty is steeped in each of these households. These young parents can only teach what they have seen, heard, and know. So poverty continues and thrives in these households. It's what they know. It's what they have always known. Why? Because they feel like if they move forward or leave what they know, they leave their family behind, and perhaps denying their heritage. No matter where you are going, if it is a new place or position, you will always have to leave something behind. My school is one of the highest most transient schools in the district. People are always moving in or moving out because of finances or striving to have a better life. I know for a fact, each time I have had to move, I usually had to make a decision on what I would take and what I would leave behind. You can't take everything. You have to decide. For me, leaving poverty and moving onward is a decision that happens in your head long before you move your body anywhere. Long before you register for your first class, you must see yourself going to school, learning, turning in homework, and passing the test. Any change starts in your head before you speak it or do it. I believe that any great achievement is NOT easy. It has its good, bad, and ugly parts but the most important thing is the goal. Where do you want to arrive? What is the goal, destination, and purpose? If it is worth it, leave some people, packages, and perspectives behind. Poverty is one of those perspectives that is hard to fight and hard to leave because to breakup with poverty you have to change your mind, motives, and movements. The goal is to be qualified, self-sufficient, whole, and walking into your destiny. What's on your mind?

Raeshal Solomon

Raeshal Solomon is a mother, author, speaker, radio host, and financial teacher, enthusiastic about combining her love of creating with her love of money management. Raeshal believes she has a knack for helping people understand the skills of money management. She is eager to share her knowledge with parents so they can teach their young children these easy to learn skills.

Raeshal writes financial literacy children's books that teach lessons like earning, saving, investing, and giving. The books are called "My Little Banker" and are for children ages 1 to 10. She says, "I am excited to change a whole generation through financial literacy." She visits elementary schools a few times a month to spread the word of financial literacy. Raeshal hosts two online radio shows, "Raeshal Speaks" and "Billionaire Minds," which you can tune to three days a week to hear her teaching about money and business.

To find out more about Raeshal visit her website http://www.mylittlebanker.com/

A Rough Start

In the winter of 1981, two young parents were awakened by the screams and cries of their new infant daughter. They had only been parents for six months, and frantically tried to find a way to stop their baby girl's tears. With no answer in sight, they rushed their baby to the ER. After hours of waiting and testing, that baby girl was diagnosed with sickle cell anemia. Hi, my name is Raeshal Solomon, and I am that baby girl.

For those who do not know what sickle cell is, it is an abnormal red blood cell disease. My red blood cells are shaped like a crescent, so they don't hold oxygen correctly. The lack of oxygen causes different levels of pain throughout the body known as a crisis. One out of every ten African Americans has some form of sickle cell. Each person with sickle cell has different things that trigger or cause their crisis. Some triggers are things like extremely hot or cold weather, first- or second-hand smoke, and physical or mental exertion.

Because people with sickle cell can't control when they get sick, it can be challenging to work a steady job. There are usually no warning signs of a crisis, and no idea of your recovery time.

I Was Young and Unwise

Although I had sickle cell, I managed to work all my high school and college years while raising my younger brother. I was 18 years old when I signed up for my first credit card. There was a group of young people offering hats, t-shirts, and sunshades to fill out an application, and I wanted a free t-shirt. In college, my mindset to money was that money could get me the things I wanted to buy. I would work and use my college loan refunds to buy stuff, including my second car. My mom had bought me a car when I was 17, but it was 20 years old and became a piece of crap. The worst part of this story was that I had grants and scholarships and didn't need the loans. No one ever taught me to manage my money; **I just did what I could to survive.**

I got my first apartment at 20 years old while still in college. In the beginning, I had many different roommates; some were dependable and some were not. After a while, I got tired of dealing with others, so I got a one bedroom and did what I could. It was small, but it was mine. My brother moved in and crashed on the couch.

I graduated college with staggering debt, and it only got worst. I got my first salary job about six months after college graduation. I was making more money than I ever had, but still no clue what to do with my money. Although I had a ton of debt, my credit score was not horrible. After about eight months of learning and focusing on my score, I increased my credit score. So, I bought my first house at age 26. Boy, was I unwise. I lost my job nine months after buying the house. It was 2007, and everyone was getting fired. The economy was crashing, and I had no backup plan, no second job, and no emergency fund. I was young, scared, and embarrassed. I didn't know anyone to ask about my current financial situation. Everyone I knew was broke, poor, or secretive about his or her money.

I applied for unemployment, and because of my sickle cell, I also applied for SSI disability. I got approved for both. Now I had income coming in, but it was barely enough to cover the mortgage. So once again I had to get roommates, and once again some were financially dependable, and some were not. For two years I cried in secret while living check to check and negotiating with the mortgage company to not foreclose.

From 2007 to 2009, I was unemployed; however, in late 2009, I went to a job fair and got a job as an assistant manager at a gas station. The pay was little, but it was a job, and it felt good to be working again. I shined at my job always doing a little extra, and my hard work paid off. A recruiter noticed me from a local restaurant chain and hired me into their management-training program. Once again, I had a great job making good money, but I didn't know what to do with it.

Six months later, the training was over and I had to move closer to my new store, so I rented my house and moved. I worked long hours. The work was hard, and I would often go to work sick, but the money was right. I met a guy while in training. He was cute, funny, and understood my busy hours. After a year of friendship, I was pregnant, but it was clear that he and I had different goals and needed to part ways.

It Does Get Better

It's 2012, and at 32 years old, I had over $400k of debt, was unemployed, single, homeless, and pregnant with my first child. This is how I got to this point. Since I was pregnant and at high risk due to the sickle cell, I had to quit my job. I had a miscarriage at six months pregnant a few years earlier and I did not want to lose another child. My boyfriend didn't want a baby, which ended our relationship. I was renting my house to good tenants, which left me homeless. Some may think I should have kicked the tenants out or moved in with them. I decided my pain was not their problem, and I couldn't afford the mortgage.

So How Did I Fix It?

I moved in with a family member to get back on my feet. I went back on Social Security Disability. I guess that was something like a backup plan. Don't get me wrong: it was hard to get. I had to fight for months to get it back. It wasn't a lot, but once my son was three months old, we moved into our own place. When my son was about 11 months, I received a call from a credit collector that left me in tears. I was angry and frustrated. At that moment, I knew my children would never know that feeling of lack. Not just lack of money, but lack of understanding money.

At that moment, I changed my mindset about money. It was no longer about what I used to buy or what I wanted. Money became a tool. A tool I was going to learned how to use. For years, I had been reading books about money, but I wasn't using what I had learned. I prayed more. I needed strength and praying was the only way I knew to get it. I grew up praying my pains away as a child, and now I was praying away a different kind of pain.

I changed the people I spent time with since many of my friends didn't know anything about money. They spent much of their time spending money they didn't have. I couldn't continue doing the same things I had done in the past; it was time for something new. I surrounded myself with people with the same goals. My church was offering a financial literacy class, so I joined it. I had the opportunity to meet new like-minded people. Honestly, I knew most of what we learned in the class, but what I realized was that I wasn't using any of it. The time for "no action" was over. I had my son and I needed to do better. I became more disciplined with my money. I did a cash audit on myself. I wrote down every dollar I spent for two months. I used those numbers to help me create my monthly budget for a snowball plan of debt reduction. I got a copy of my credit report so I could call the collectors and negotiate payment plans. I changed my shopping habits, stopped carrying debit cards, and for a while paid for things with cash only. I still read every book, online article, and listened to every podcast I can find about money.

Now

I started writing children's books to teach kids financial literacy. I use fun and colorful stories that they read and learn a lesson about money. I wrote a series of books entitled "My Little Banker." I travel around the country teaching kids about money, and I teach parents how to teach their children about money. I use my skills to teach my kids about money as well. I am happy to be living and working in my purpose to teach people from my pain. Money is no longer something I don't understand. Now money is a tool I use to grow my career and my legacy.

<u>Sherry Thompson</u>

Sherry Cockerham Thompson, EdS, is a former community college counselor/administrator with over 20 years' experience helping students achieve their dreams. She herself was once a non-traditional college student, having returned to college at the age of 30 when she was a single mom with three small boys under the age of five. As she helped students work toward achieving their dreams, she always remembered what it was like to be a scared college freshman living well below the poverty line. The road to that first, two-year degree was hard, but she believed her education was a way out of poverty for her and her children. She struggled, working part time and going to school full time, but she knew that someday she could help other women and make a difference in her community. She completed an associate of arts in college transfer from Wilkes Community College and then transferred to Appalachian State University and completed a bachelor of social work degree. Later, she got a master's degree in college student development, concentration counseling and an Ed.S. in higher education, both from Appalachian State University.

Thompson now is an entrepreneur and enjoys helping others pursue their dreams through her writing and entrepreneurship. She enjoys her family time, biking, hiking, swimming, and traveling adventures with her husband, Jim Thompson. Her sons Michael, Matthew, and Marcus Miller are now grown, with families of their own, and she has five grandchildren, Kaylee, Levi, Keegan, Morgan, and Quentin. They are her pride and joy, and she strives to help them dream BIG DREAMS and believe in themselves, just as she hopes this chapter will inspire you to BELIEVE that ANYTHING is possible with hard work and commitment to YOURSELF and YOUR DREAMS.

The Smell of Poverty

Poverty is a complex problem, often thought of in connection with inner cities, but it's all too common in rural Appalachia. I was born in the Blue Ridge Mountains of North Carolina, but my parents moved to a city in the foothills when I was two, so they could find better jobs. I am one of three children, and my parents both worked as long as they were able. We always had a home, but we were one paycheck from falling off a cliff. Things would get tough if my mom or dad would get sick or was temporarily unemployed.

At 19, I left home to become an independent woman. Because my parents always stressed hard work, I had two or three jobs while trying to go to college. Unsure of my major and coming from a family that did not stress education, I eventually dropped out.

On the rebound from a long-term relationship, I met my "Prince Charming" and we got married. I didn't understand what real poverty was like until we moved back to the mountain county where he and I were both born. It was then that his alcoholism and drug abuse became apparent.

After many long years of trying to change this man, I realized it was me that changed and not in good ways. I found myself living in the middle of Appalachia, with no public transportation, no car, and no job to be found. My confidence, self-esteem, and ability to dream were gone. I had three sons, and we lived in a little shack of a house with no insulation and limited heat. Many times our water would be frozen in the winter. I was walking to my aunt's house for water to heat on the wood stove so that I could bathe the babies. There was always stress. There was always worry, fighting, and unhappiness.

Our food sometimes came from food pantries. This food came in dented cans or was outdated. Later, we got food stamps and though I was a proud woman who hated asking for help, my pride couldn't stand in the way of my kids getting food. I'll never forget applying for assistance; my husband was working and because of that, we didn't qualify for public assistance. I explained that he didn't bring the money home to me and the kids and that he needed treatment for his addictions. But the only answer I got was that he couldn't live in the home and we get assistance. So I asked him to leave, but I was still totally dependent on him or family for transportation. Even getting to the store or laundry was a challenge. It was a very scary time, and every day I was scared I couldn't buy food, wash clothes, or even have basic toiletries.

Eventually, I was able to buy a car from a friend for $100. It ran great, but it had a hole in the floor big enough that one of my kids could have fallen through if they had gotten out of their car seats. I found a job in a group home, helping people with disabilities. My kids having a father was important to me, so I took my husband back several times, each time hoping for change and that he could keep his promises — but he couldn't. I could only change me. Eventually, I started back to college to finish the degree I'd started. This was really the beginning of me finding myself and believing in myself. Until this point, I felt like a total failure. The only reason that I kept going was those three little smiles that desperately needed me to find a way for them. They were my "why" and my cheerleaders.

Working and going to school while solo parenting meant that I had very little time for anything else. I didn't date or see friends. I had a schedule for them in the evenings to get dinner, baths, homework done, and a bedtime story. They went to bed early by 8 p.m., because by 8:30 p.m. I had to be studying. I would do homework and study until midnight most nights. If I had a test the next day, I would be up by 4:30 or 5 a.m., studying again. I thankfully found a friend who would drive to school and I would pay for gas because her car was much cheaper to drive than mine. I wouldn't have made it through this period without friends who became like family and pitched in to help us.

Those friends became priceless to me, since not everyone understood my goals. When I started to college, my mother was very upset with me. She couldn't see the benefit to my going to college and thought that I was crazy for making that choice when I had three kids to feed. Thankfully, there were programs in place at the time that helped with transportation expenses, food stamps, and a small monthly check of $196. That AFDC check, plus my Pell grant, and part-time wages let us get by. We didn't have a lot of extra money, but I had my sights set on a time in the future when I could use my life experiences to help others. I majored in social work because I did want to make a difference for women. That gave me hope and a sense of purpose. After a while, my purpose drove my desire and kept me moving forward.

A lot of people who could have been helpers in Social Services weren't; they challenged the "reasonableness" of my plan to go to college. Some would make rude comments about how they wished they could go to school but didn't have the opportunity. Of course, I did notice that they had nice shiny diamonds and cars, meaning someone was probably buying those diamonds and there were two incomes in the family. It was a matter of their priorities and mine being different. I'm only sharing this because society isn't very supportive of families in poverty, and everyone needs to find their own support system, if you don't have one in place already. You need a team to help you reach your goals. I'm grateful every day for the people in the agency and community who believed in me and encouraged me.

I'll admit that I had made a mistake by marrying someone who wasn't prepared for the responsibilities of a family and I had no real understanding of addiction at the time. I had no idea how short his sobriety would be when he married me. But I was willing to sacrifice anything that I needed to in order to reach my goal: a job with a salary above poverty level. And

NEVER having to pay for my food with food stamps again.

Finally after four LONG, HARD years, I finally made it. I graduated and got a job helping others. I was fortunate to get a job in education and training with the Department of Labor and later a community college. I really loved helping first generation college students like myself, and I always liked sharing my story with our single-parenting students so that they knew, that I knew what their struggle was like.

Because the resources aren't available in the same way today in terms of childcare, transportation, etc., I decided to become an entrepreneur, so that I can help mommas build a business online and be present with their kids. This is an opportunity that the Internet has opened for families that our family didn't have. Just like my education shaped my thinking and our family's future, so has entrepreneurship. I love sharing those valuable lessons with others so that they can soar right to the top. Today more than ever, I believe that women deserve the independence and time freedom to build a business around their kids' schedules.

I'm grateful for my journey through poverty. It gave me a better understanding of what millions of people face every day. It also helped me to understand the oppressive obstacles and the power of a daily practice moving forward one more step towards the dream that you hold in your mind. You and your family are worth your fight, don't give up. Find your dream, your tribe, and your grit for your journey, moving forward one day at a time towards the life that you deserve.

You can learn more online at www.sharingthrive.com on my blog "Strong Self-Image Through a Shattered Lens."

www.ingramcontent.com/pod-product-compliance
Lightning Source LLC
Chambersburg PA
CBHW050405030726
47503CB00006B/2024